Bulldogs

and Other Nonsporting Dogs

Editorial:
Editor in Chief: Paul A. Kobasa
Project Manager: Cassie Mayer
Writer: Ana Deboo
Researcher: Cheryl Graham
Manager, Contracts & Compliance
  (Rights & Permissions): Loranne K. Shields
Indexer: David Pofelski

Graphics and Design:
Manager: Tom Evans
Coordinator, Design Development and
  Production: Brenda B. Tropinski
Designer: Matthew Carrington
Cartographer: John Rejba
Contributing Photographs Editor: Clover Morell

Pre-Press and Manufacturing:
Director: Carma Fazio
Manufacturing Manager:
  Steven K. Hueppchen
Production/Technology Manager:
  Anne Fritzinger

**For information about other World Book publications,
visit our Web site at http://www.worldbookonline.com
or call 1-800-WORLDBK (967-5325).**

**For information about sales to schools and libraries,
call 1-800-975-3250 (United States),
or 1-800-837-5365 (Canada).**

World Book, Inc.
233 N. Michigan Avenue
Chicago, IL 60601
U.S.A.

Library of Congress Cataloging-in-Publication Data

Bulldogs and other nonsporting dogs.
    p. cm. — (World Book's animals of the world)
  Includes index.
  Summary: "An introduction to bulldogs and other nonsporting
dogs, presented in a highly illustrated, question-and-answer
format. Features include fun facts, glossary, resource list, index,
and scientific classification list"—Provided by publisher.
  ISBN 978-0-7166-1371-8
  1. Bulldog—Juvenile literature. 2. Dogs—Juvenile literature.
I. World Book, Inc.
SF429.B85B86 2010
636.72—dc22
                    2009024240

World Book's Animals of the World
Set 6: ISBN: 978-0-7166-1365-7
Printed in China by Leo Paper Products LTD., Heshan, Guangdong
1st printing November 2009

Picture Acknowledgments: Cover: © Adriano Bacchella, Nature Picture Library; © Jay M. Schulz, Dreamstime;
© Kris Hanke, iStockphoto; © Degtyaryov Andrey Leonidovich, Shutterstock; © Shutterstock.

© blickwinkel/Alamy Images 27, 55; © Corbis Premium RF/Alamy Images 57; © Mark Scheuern, Alamy Images 53;
© UpperCut Images/Alamy Images 19; © WoodyStock/Alamy Images 51; © Barbara Von Hoffman, Animals Animals 23;
© Dreamstime 7, 17, 29, 31, 33, 43, 45, 49, 61; © iStockphoto 35, 47; © David Schmidt, Masterfile 59; © Adriano
Bacchella, Nature Picture Library 37; © Jeff Greenberg, PhotoEdit 15, 39; © Frank Siteman, PhotoEdit 41; © Shutterstock
9; © age fotostock/SuperStock 21; © Flirt/SuperStock 25.

Illustrations: WORLD BOOK illustration by Roberta Polfus 13.

World Book's Animals of the World

Bulldogs
and Other Nonsporting Dogs

WORLD
BOOK

a Scott Fetzer company
Chicago
www.worldbookonline.com

Contents

What Is a Nonsporting Dog?

Many countries have organizations that group dogs according to their traits or to the work the dogs originally performed. For example, the hound group includes dogs that were once commonly used for hunting. But some dog breeds don't fit well in any of the standard groups. The American Kennel Club, or AKC, includes these dogs in a nonsporting group, a collection of breeds that don't fit anywhere else. Nonsporting dogs were bred for various purposes—to hunt, help on farms or in monasteries, live on boats, act as guards, fight, and keep people company. Many were multitalented and did more than one job.

Breed groups differ according to each organization. In the United Kingdom, for example, the Kennel Club (KC) category "utility dogs" contains most breeds in the AKC's nonsporting group. The Australian National Kennel Council (ANKC) and the Canadian Kennel Club (CKC) both have a nonsporting category that includes most of the dogs in the AKC's nonsporting group.

A bulldog

7

How Did Breeds of Nonsporting Dogs Develop?

A breed is a group of animals that have the same type of ancestors. The nonsporting breeds come from all over the world. The Chinese shar-pei *(shahr pay)*, Finnish spitz, Tibetan spaniel, and Tibetan terrier were bred in the countries mentioned in their names. The Lhasa apso *(LAH suh AP soh)* is also from Tibet. Boston terriers were developed in Boston, Massachusetts—but French bulldogs are from England. Each of these breeds has its own unique history.

The names of some nonsporting dogs can be misleading. For example, the Tibetan terrier is not related to true terriers, while the Boston terrier can count real terriers as ancestors. The Tibetan spaniel is not a true spaniel and was not used in hunting (which is what spaniels were bred for). The Tibetan spaniel and terrier breeds are at least 2,000 years old.

You will find more about other nonsporting breeds on pages 42 through 51.

A Chinese shar-pei

A Tibetan terrier

A French bulldog

A Tibetan spaniel

When and Where Did the Bulldog Breed First Appear?

The bulldog comes from the United Kingdom—it is also known as the English or British bulldog. It is a descendant of larger dogs that, long ago, acted as butchers' assistants by helping to hold bulls still so they could be killed for meat. Eventually, the dogs became more popular as contestants in a bloody sport called bullbaiting—a fight to the death between a chained-up bull and a group of dogs. Breeders developed traits in the dogs that would make them especially good fighters (see page 12).

Bullbaiting was popular entertainment for centuries. Finally, in 1835, the British Parliament outlawed it. After that, people kept breeding the dog because they liked its looks. They aimed to make it a friendly companion dog. Now bulldogs, which once had to be vicious to do their jobs, are known for their gentleness.

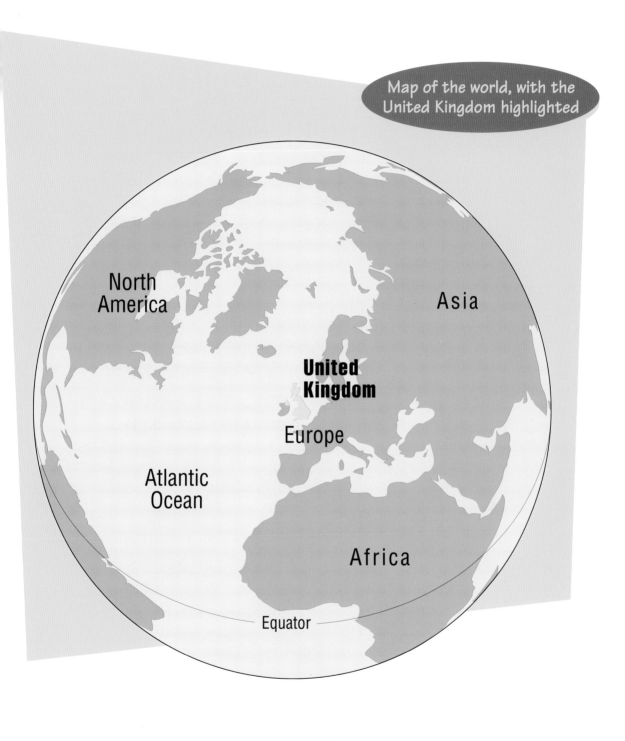

North
America

Asia

United
Kingdom

Europe

Atlantic
Ocean

Africa

Equator

What Does a Bulldog Look Like?

The bulldog is a medium-sized dog with a thick, heavy, low-slung body. Its distinctive features played a role in its former job of fighting bulls. It has a large mouth with a jutting lower jaw that can bite and grip tightly. Its short, snub nose allowed it to breathe as it hung on to the bull. The wrinkled skin on its face directed the bull's blood away from the dog's eyes. Its short legs allowed it to dart under the bull to attack. Its broad, muscular chest shows its strength, which was obviously important with a bull as its opponent.

The bulldog has a short coat of fur that can be fawn-colored, red, or brindled, and is either solid or patched. It stands about 14 inches (36 centimeters) tall at the shoulder and weighs up to 50 pounds (23 kilograms).

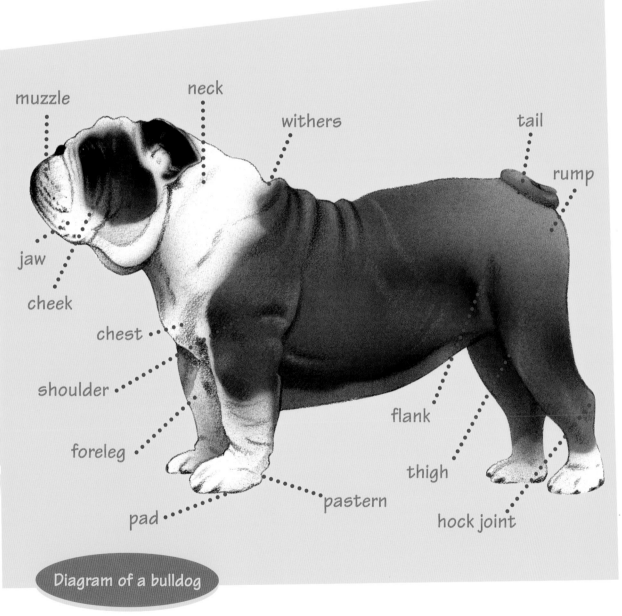

muzzle

neck

withers

tail

rump

jaw

cheek

chest

shoulder

flank

foreleg

thigh

pad

pastern

hock joint

Diagram of a bulldog

13

What Kind of Personality Might a Bulldog Have?

Despite their history as fighters and their appearance, bulldogs tend to be mild-mannered and calm. They get along with cats and most other dogs and may even become good friends with them, but they are usually most interested in human affection. Bulldogs love attention and cuddling. Heavy as they are, they even sometimes try to imitate lapdogs.

Like their fierce ancestors, bulldogs can be brave to the point of risking their lives to protect their owners. They are also loyal. They tend to be gentle and patient with very young children.

Bulldogs prefer to be inactive, so be sure to give your bulldog moderate exercise so it does not become overweight.

Bulldogs are lovable family dogs.

Is a Bulldog the Dog for You?

Bulldogs have a lot going for them as companions. Since they do not need much exercise, bulldogs can live happily in small apartments, or with people who cannot take long, vigorous walks. In these ways, bulldogs are "easy" pets, but there are other things to consider.

Bulldogs require much attention and affection, or they will be unhappy. They also should be indoor dogs. Their short fur does not protect them from cold or bad weather and, when it is warm, they overheat quickly.

Their oddly shaped heads can cause other problems, too. Bulldogs can be extremely slobbery. Their snub noses make them more likely to snore and to breathe heavily in general. But as many bulldog owners will tell you, their friendly, lovable nature makes up for such issues.

A panting bulldog

What Should You Look for When Choosing a Bulldog Puppy?

Once your family has done research and decides to get a bulldog puppy, it is important to find a good breeder. (See page 64 for good places to start investigating.) This means someone whose main concerns are producing healthy bulldog puppies and placing them in good homes. Good breeders will ask you a lot of questions before putting a dog in your care. They will also know their dogs' personalities well enough to recommend which puppies might suit your family best.

Puppies should be at least eight weeks old before they are taken from their mother, and they should be comfortable around people. It is usually best to choose one that seems interested in meeting you and acts cheerful and curious. You will have your pet for many years, so it is important to choose a puppy with which you and your family feel a connection.

Bulldog puppies

Should You Get an Older Bulldog Instead of a Puppy?

True, if you get a full-grown bulldog, you miss the cute puppy antics. But you will likely also miss cleaning up messes and dealing with babyish troublemaking. An adult dog should already be housebroken—that is, trained to go to the bathroom outside or in the proper place. You will also have a better idea of an older dog's personality and things like whether it is going to drool a lot or only a little. Plus, adult bulldogs are known for acting like big puppies anyway.

One risk with an adult dog is that it might have had bad experiences that result in behavior problems, or it may have trouble adjusting to your household routine for some reason. If possible, arrange to have a test period with an adult dog to see how it fits in with your family.

An older bulldog

Should You Consider a Rescue Bulldog?

Bulldogs are popular pets. At times, they make the top-ten lists of most commonly owned dogs in the United States and the United Kingdom. That means more people may get one because it is fashionable. Then they discover it is too much of a commitment. Too often, they abandon the dog.

There are special organizations dedicated to rescuing purebred dogs that were abandoned, got lost, or had loving owners who could not keep them for some reason. They work to place the dogs with new families.

If a puppy isn't the right choice for your family, you may want to consider getting a bulldog from a rescue organization. You can do a good deed by giving one of those rescue dogs a happy home. See the Web sites on page 64 to get started finding a rescue organization near you.

Bulldogs at a shelter

What Does a Bulldog Eat?

Giving your dog the right kind and amount of food is an important part of keeping it healthy. Dogs need different nutrients, or nourishing things, than people do. That's why it is best for a dog to eat dog food. Commercially produced dog foods are a good way to provide balanced nutrition.

Compared with other dogs, bulldogs have sensitive digestive systems. When something does not agree with them, it can cause stomach problems, and it is common for them to pass gas. You may have to experiment to find what food works best for your bulldog. Your veterinarian may also suggest dog foods that are right for your dog.

Many experts agree that it is fine to give your dog occasional treats of human food, as long as your dog is keeping a healthy weight. Some foods, such as chocolate, grapes and raisins, sugarless candies, and onions, are poisonous to any dog. Research this thoroughly before feeding your dog anything other than dog food.

A bulldog eating

Where Should a Bulldog Sleep?

Bulldogs are noisy sleepers and are likely to disturb your rest. Most snore, and their regular breathing is not quiet either. For all these reasons, it may be best to have your dog sleep in its own space rather than on your bed. A dog that gets used to sleeping with you will not understand if you change your mind about this later on, or if you occasionally want to be alone. If you establish from the start that your bed is off limits, and enforce the rule consistently, there will never be misunderstandings over sleeping arrangements.

Many dog experts believe that a dog should have its own metal cage. You can place a cozy bed inside the cage. Various dog beds are also available. Bulldogs like to chew on things, such as wood, rugs, and wicker, so keep those items out of the cage. Provide plenty of chew toys in the cage.

A bulldog in its bed

27

How Do You Groom a Bulldog?

Bulldogs have extremely short hair, which makes them easier to groom than many dogs. Still, bulldogs do have several grooming needs. Brushing your dog regularly will keep its skin in good condition and prevent the dog from shedding in your house. Also, dirt collects in a bulldog's many wrinkles and around the tail. You should clean the dog's face and tail well with a damp cloth or unscented baby wipe every day. This can also keep tear stains from forming around the eyes.

If you groom your dog several times a week, it will likely not need to be bathed unless it gets especially dirty or smelly. Because of a bulldog's small size, you may be able to fit your pet in a large kitchen sink or a bathtub to do this job. Bulldogs can get chilled easily, so bathe your pet only when it's warm outside, and dry it thoroughly.

It is important to keep a bulldog's nails trimmed— overgrown nails can interfere with its walking. Some adults clip the nails with special dog clippers, while others use a special grinder. You can also have a professional dog groomer perform this task.

Bathing a bulldog

What About Training a Bulldog?

If you've ever been to a park, you've likely witnessed all kinds of dog behavior. Some dogs walk calmly alongside their owners, while others tug at the end of the leash and seem to be taking their owners for a walk! Training your dog from an early age can help ensure that your dog is well behaved most of the time.

Bulldogs have a reputation for being independent-minded—some people go so far as to say stubborn. This does not mean that bulldogs cannot be trained. In fact, such a big, powerful dog must be trained so you can stay in control. The process may take patience, though. Start with the young puppy if possible and give lots of praise, never punishment. You may wish to enroll in dog training classes to learn special tips and techniques.

At a minimum, your bulldog needs to know how to obey the command "no," how to behave on a leash, and how to sit and stay. Teaching it other tricks will give you a chance to appreciate its clownish sense of humor.

A bulldog learning
how to sit

31

What Kinds of Exercise or Play Are Needed?

Bulldogs do not need vigorous exercise to keep fit. They must, of course, do something to keep their hearts healthy and to avoid gaining weight. Moderate choices like taking walks in your neighborhood or playing for a while in the yard or indoors are best.

It is important to protect bulldogs from extreme temperatures. In hot weather, especially, they can easily overexert themselves, and this can be dangerous, so be watchful. Take them outside early or late in the day on hot days.

Also, though some bulldogs love the idea of swimming, they are not strong swimmers. They are so muscular and heavy that their bodies tend to sink, and their short noses are difficult to hold above the water. Never let your bulldog spend time unsupervised around a swimming pool or any body of water.

A bulldog on a walk

How Do Bulldogs Like to Play?

Though bulldogs are not athletic, they are playful, especially when they are young. Most enjoy romping with other dogs as well as frolicking with their human friends.

The bulldog is not a breed known for fetching balls, but they do like to chase them—and some will even learn to bring the ball back to you. Bulldogs also like playing tug-of-war.

When you go outside with your bulldog, bring water and offer it regular drinks. Remember that bulldogs can get overheated. Do not expect your bulldog to do much running. On a leash, walking is the best pace. When your bulldog plays, it will run around but may tire quickly. Then it is time to go home for a nice, long nap.

This bulldog is ready to play!

35

Should You Breed Your Bulldog?

For nearly everyone, it is better to spay or neuter your pet so the animal will not be able to produce puppies. (A vet spays female dogs and neuters male dogs.) The fact that there are so many homeless dogs on the street and in rescue shelters shows that the dog population is greater than the number of people willing to adopt pets. In addition, breeding bulldogs is more difficult than breeding other kinds of dog. The parent bulldogs must be carefully chosen to reduce the likelihood of passing on inherited problems to the puppies.

Because bulldog puppies have large heads but the mother has narrow hips, most bulldog puppies are delivered by cesarean section, rather than naturally. This is an operation in which the mother's abdomen is cut open and the puppies are removed. This birth process has to be closely supervised by a veterinarian.

A mother bulldog and one of her puppies

Are There Special Organizations for Bulldog Owners?

Bulldog owners are often quite enthusiastic about the breed. Many use the affectionate breed nickname "bullies" and call themselves "bulldoggers." There are both local and national clubs for bulldog enthusiasts to join so they can support the breed and participate in events starring bulldogs.

In the United States, the main organization devoted to bulldogs is the Bulldog Club of America. In the United Kingdom, there are the Bulldog Club Inc. and the British Bulldog Club. All three of these groups have been around for a long time—they were founded in the late 1800's. There are also bulldog-oriented groups in Australia and Canada.

Use the links on page 64 to find out about local bulldog clubs near where you live and the events that they sponsor.

A bulldog and its companion

How Do Bulldogs Help People?

The bulldog's greatest talent—the skill it has been bred for since its bull-fighting days ended—is companionship. Bulldogs love to keep people company. You might say they help people by being their friends. The bulldog has been one of the most popular breeds for many years, which suggests that they are pretty successful at it.

One great way for your bulldog to help people is to be a therapy dog. These dogs visit people in hospitals and other care facilities to cheer them up. Children and elderly patients in particular benefit from this. An organization called Therapy Dogs International offers certification for this type of training.

40

A therapy dog

41

What Are Some Other Nonsporting Dog Breeds?

There are 16 breeds in the AKC's nonsporting dog group. Two of them have bulldog ancestors: French bulldogs and Boston terriers. French bulldogs were developed by British lacemakers in the 1800's to be lapdogs and were later taken to France.

Three breeds are spitzes, a type of dog known for having a pointy nose and ears (spitz means "pointed" in German): the American Eskimo Dog, Finnish spitz, and keeshond.

The keeshond (from the Netherlands), the bichon frise (from the Mediterranean), and the schipperke (from Belgium) were popular with sailors. Schipperke means "little captain." Three of the breeds were popular with Tibetan monks: the Lhasa apso, Tibetan spaniel, and Tibetan terrier.

Four other nonsporting dog breeds are described on the following pages.

A Boston terrier

What Is a Chow Chow?

The chow chow is an ancient spitz-type dog from China, one of the breeds that first descended from wolves. It performed various jobs—hunting, pulling sleds, guarding homes—and was killed for its meat or for its thick fur in some parts of Asia.

Chow chows are big dogs that weigh up to 75 pounds (34 kilograms). The cream, cinnamon, and red ones, especially, can look a bit like lions. They may also be white, blue-gray, or black. The breed has an unusual bluish-black tongue; its relative, the Chinese shar-pei (also in the nonsporting group), is the only other dog with this feature.

Fairly reserved with strangers but loyal to their families, chow chows may become especially attached to one person. They are considered strong, active, and intelligent dogs. However, they can be stubborn and aloof toward their owners.

Because of their thick coats, chow chows need regular grooming and bathing.

A chow chow

What Is a Dalmatian?

Dalmatians are bright white dogs with dramatic black or liver-colored spots that are familiar to everybody. They are famous as mascots for fire departments and as stars of the Walt Disney movie, *101 Dalmatians.* They are tall, slender, intelligent dogs that can perform all sorts of jobs, and they are especially talented at distance running and getting along with horses. Often called coach dogs, Dalmatians used to run alongside their owners' horse-drawn coaches and carriages, both for protection and for show.

Though this old breed is named after a region in Croatia called Dalmatia, it probably does not come from there. No one knows for sure where or how it first became a breed.

Dalmatians are usually good around people and are considered a fine family pet. Their high level of energy means that they must get plenty of exercise every day.

46

A Dalmatian

47

What Is a Poodle?

The poodle is an intelligent, athletic breed that is known for its ability to learn and follow commands. The classic poodle haircut might look a little silly, but those puffs originally had a practical use. Early poodles were retrievers, who specialized in bringing fallen waterbirds back to hunters. The haircut was short in some spots, so swimming was easier, and long in others, to keep the dog warm.

Poodles come in a range of colors, including white, black, apricot, and gray. There are two poodle sizes in the nonsporting group: standard, or over 15 inches (38 centimeters) tall at the shoulder, and miniature, no shorter than 10 inches (25 centimeters). The toy dog group includes an even smaller poodle.

The poodle was probably developed in Germany during the 1500's, even though it is often associated with France. It became so popular in France that some people call these dogs French poodles.

A standard poodle

49

What Is a Shiba Inu?

The shiba inu *(SHEE buh EE noo)* is a small dog that was originally bred in Japan for hunting birds and other small wild game, as well as boar, deer, and bear. The name means "brushwood dog," perhaps because the dog was good at running through underbrush when hunting. This breed is thought to be as old as the chow chow. It almost became extinct during the hardships experienced by Japan during World War II (1939-1945). Since then, it has become the most popular dog in Japan and its popularity is spreading to other countries, including the United States.

Shiba inus are less than 16 inches (40 centimeters) tall at the shoulder and weigh about 25 pounds (11 kilograms). They have a double coat of fur and can be mostly red or black, or a cream color called sesame. They are known for acting rather catlike and being less apt to bark than making a yodeling sound.

A shiba inu

51

What Is a Dog Show Like?

Dog shows bring people together so they can show off their purebred dogs and share information. Most shows are sponsored by such organizations as the American Kennel Club. Crufts, sponsored by the Kennel Club in the United Kingdom, is the largest dog show in the world. The largest show in the United States is the Westminster Kennel Club Dog Show in New York. Australian dog owners can compete in Royal Shows, which happen in different places all over the country.

The main events at many dog shows are conformation competitions, in which the best example of a breed is chosen based on the dog's appearance. Contests that show the dogs in action, such as obedience and agility trials, are also popular.

Show bulldogs are expected to be strong, kind, and brave without showing any tendency toward aggressiveness. An ideal bulldog should have muscular, wide shoulders, short, sturdy limbs, and a very large head.

Bulldogs at a dog show

Are There Dangers to Dogs Around the Home?

Some things in your home are dangerous to your dog. Puppies are the most likely to run into trouble. Make sure you know what foods can be harmful and store them somewhere safe. Plants can be toxic, too. Remove poisonous houseplants from your home or put them well out of your dog's reach. Also, avoid planting toxic plants in your yard.

Some dogs like to chew things, and many have been injured gnawing on power cords. Even a toy made for dogs may be dangerous if the dog can break pieces off that might cause choking. Evaluate anything in your home for safety before allowing your dog access to it.

Consult the sources on page 64 to begin researching how to dog-proof your home.

A bulldog at home

What Are Some Common Signs of Illness?

Purebred dogs may have health problems caused by their breeding. This may be because their parents were too closely related, or breeders may have worked too much to emphasize some physical traits and lost other important qualities. For example, dogs with mashed-in faces often have breathing problems and cannot easily cool off by panting, as other dogs do. The bulldog, chow chow, Boston terrier, French bulldog, and Lhasa apso are breeds that are prone to breathing problems.

Bulldogs were originally bred to have a high pain threshold, and they still tend to act as if they do not feel discomfort. It can be hard to tell when any dog is sick, but this makes it especially difficult.

Any change in your dog's behavior can be a sign of illness, so be sure to observe your dog closely every day. Common signs of illness include a change in appetite, fever, vomiting, diarrhea, a dry nose, a dull coat, bald patches, unusual discharge from a dog's nose, ears, or eyes; and redness of the eyes.

Any time your family suspects that your dog might be ill, it's best to check with your vet promptly.

A tired bulldog

What Routine Veterinary Care Is Needed?

A bulldog lives an average of eight years, but if you get a dog from a good breeder and provide the medical care it needs, you may be able to keep your friend around for longer. If possible, find a veterinarian who knows about bulldogs and their needs. Your family could also research bulldog health so you can be on the alert for the problems that might come up.

Your dog should go to the veterinarian every year for a checkup. The doctor will do a physical examination and give vaccinations and shots according to an established schedule. A vaccine is a special medicine that protects people, dogs, and other animals from certain serious diseases. You might need to have your dog's teeth cleaned or get advice about how to help it maintain a healthy weight.

A bulldog getting a checkup

What Are Your Responsibilities as an Owner?

Ages ago, when dogs were still wolves, they could take care of themselves. But now that they have been domesticated for thousands of years and bred into all kinds of specialized forms, most dogs could no longer survive in the wild—the bulldog definitely could not.

When you make a dog part of your family, you commit to giving it food, shelter, medical care, love, and anything else needed to ensure the dog's well-being. You must be sure that your dog receives all the necessary vaccinations (shots) to protect against diseases, and have the dog spayed or neutered so it does not produce unwanted puppies.

You should also remember to be a good citizen, picking up your dog's messes when you are out and about, and training it so it does not misbehave. It can be hard work at times, but your dog will repay your efforts with devotion and love.

It is important to
give your dog much love
and attention.

61

Nonsporting Dog Fun Facts

→ Sigmund Freud, the Austrian psychoanalyst, had several chow chows. One of them, Jo-Fi, sat in on Freud's sessions with patients, because he thought the dog could help them feel more at ease. An added benefit was that Jo-Fi always told Freud when the session was over by walking to the door.

→ Many Dalmatians have a facial expression like a smile, which they make when they are happy. It can be a little scary if you do not know what it is, because it looks almost like a fierce snarl. But once you get used to a Dalmatian's smile, you will start to look forward to seeing it.

→ Winston Churchill, prime minister of the United Kingdom during World War II (1939-1945), was nicknamed "the British bulldog" because of his looks and reputation for being stubborn and tough. He never owned a bulldog—but he did have two beloved miniature poodles, Rufus I and Rufus II (after Rufus I died).

→ The keeshond played a part in 1700's Dutch politics. A party called the Patriots rebelled against the ruler of the time, the prince of Orange. One of the Patriots' leaders, Kees de Gyselaer, made his dog their mascot. Now the breed is the national dog of the Netherlands.

Glossary

ancestor An animal from which another animal is directly descended. Usually, *ancestor* is used to refer to an animal more removed than a parent or grandparent.

breed To produce animals by carefully selecting and mating them for certain traits. Also, a group of animals having the same type of ancestors.

breeder A person who breeds animals.

brindled A streaky or speckled pattern of dark fur mixed with gray or brownish fur.

cesarean section An operation to remove babies from a pregnant mother when she cannot give birth naturally.

domesticated Adapted over thousands of years to live with human beings.

fawn-colored Pale yellowish or grayish brown.

groom To take care of an animal, for example, by combing, brushing, or trimming its coat.

neuter To operate on a male animal to make it unable to produce young.

pain threshold The point at which pain begins to be felt. An animal is said to have a high pain threshold if it takes a lot of physical stimulation for it to notice the discomfort.

purebred An animal whose parents are known to have both belonged to one breed.

shed To throw off or lose hair, skin, fur, or other body covering.

spay To operate on a female animal to make it unable to have young.

trait A feature or characteristic particular to an animal or breed of animals.

Index

(**Boldface** indicates a photo, map, or illustration.)

For more information about bulldogs and other nonsporting dogs, try these resources:

Books:

Bulldogs by Lynn M. Stone (Rourke Publishing, 2007)

The Complete Dog Book for Kids by the American Kennel Club (Howell Book House, 1996)

Dogs by Dr. Bruce Fogle (DK Publishing, 2006)

Web sites:

The American Kennel Club
http://www.akc.org

Australian National Kennel Council
http://www.ankc.org.au

British Bulldog Club
www.britishbulldogclub.co.uk

Bulldog Club of America
http://thebca.org

Bulldog Club of America Rescue Network
http://www.rescuebulldogs.org

The Bulldog Club Inc.
http://www.bulldog-inc.om

Canadian Kennel Club
http://www.ckc.ca/en/

Kennel Club (United Kingdom)
http://www.thekennelclub.org.uk

Dog Classification

Scientists classify animals by placing them into groups. The animal kingdom is a group that contains all the world's animals. Phylum, class, order, and family are smaller groups. Each phylum contains many classes. A class contains orders, an order contains families, and a family contains genuses. One or more species belong to each genus. Each species has its own scientific name. Here is how the animals in this book fit into this system.

Animals with backbones and their relatives (Phylum Chordata)
Mammals (Class Mammalia)
Carnivores (Order Carnivora)

Dogs and their relatives (Family Canidae)

Domestic dog . . . . *Canis familiaris*